Building Trust and Being Trustworthy

The Components of Trust and Trustworthiness:

Quintessential Leader Traits You Can't Lead Without

Table of Contents

Chapter 1: Trust and Trustworthiness – A Quintessential Leader Trait

Trust and trustworthiness - one is from others to us while the other is our state of being - are core quintessential leader traits. This book defines the components a quintessential leader must have in order to have trust and be trustworthy.

Since trust is, both from us and toward us, a by-product of being trustworthy, I want to look in today's post at a brief summary of characteristics - I plan to discuss most, if not all, of these individually in depth in upcoming posts - that make a leader trustworthy.

There are two main components of trustworthiness. One is character and the second is competency. If either of these is missing or deficient, there is no trustworthiness.

Character, which Steven M. R. Covey (*Speed of Trust*) summarizes as doing the right thing, is who we are, while competency, which Covey summarizes as doing things the right way, is what we do. Character, good or bad, is the first and last impression the people our lives intersect with carry with them. Competency is harder to gauge and is something that is revealed more slowly over time. As a leader, I often made hiring decisions based on character rather than competency, knowing that character is usually set long before a person ever darkens the door of an office building, and if it's bad or deficient, it will be difficult, if not impossible, to change. Competency, on the other hand, can be taught and can be learned at any stage in life.

So what character traits engender others' trust in us and establish us as being trustworthy, and therefore, quintessential leaders?

- Honesty - Being truthful in every aspect of life
- Integrity - Possessing and adhering to morally-right and ethical principles no matter what
- Fairness - Treating all people the same way and holding them to the same standards
- Respect - Showing care and concern for and kindness to all people
- Accountability - Taking full responsibility for what is within your control and expecting the same from your team
- Sincerity - Being genuine, authentic, and real
- Focus on adding value - Ensuring that you give as much or more than you get in all relationships
- Right wrongs - Being willing to quickly fix problems and mistakes
- Moral courage - Doing the right thing all the time

- Consistency - Being the same at all times in who you are, how you are, and what you are
- Trust - Showing others that you trust them
- Setting boundaries - Establishing what is acceptable and unacceptable and adhering to it with no exceptions
- Raising the bar - Holding yourself to a higher standard of conduct at all times
In the area of competencies that are required for the Quintessential Leader trait of trustworthiness, some of these come naturally, but others don't because they require us to put our egos away and that's is a hard thing for us all to do sometimes, but it is absolutely necessary if we are going to be trustworthy. These competencies are:
- Listening - Being willing to hear the good, the bad, and the ugly…even if it's about you
- Taking criticism well - Learning to handle all criticism with grace instead of defensiveness
- Responsiveness - Being quick to do what you say you're going to do and to deal correctly with issues, problems, mistakes, surprises, and needs
- Reliability - Being dependable all the time
- Being present - Being 100% - no multitasking allowed! -engaged with people who are communicating with you

The next chapters will look at most, if not all, of these individual character and competency traits in detail and will include "this-is-what-this-looks-like-in-practice" examples. Sometimes unless we see some of these things in action, they can seem like lofty and noble, but unattainable traits. They are not. But they all require a full investment and commitment all of the time, and that can be a real challenge for all of us.

But it is the only way to really gain others' trust and become trustworthy, so this is one challenge I personally am committed to. I hope that as we go through this series together, the value - and the peace of mind that comes from being trustworthy - of making that commitment will become apparent and compelling.

Chapter 2: The Honesty Component of Trust and Trustworthiness

Most of us in the 21st Century have been conditioned by society and experience to be skeptics about everything. We live in a dishonest world. I personally believe that is one of the underlying reasons why the key tenants of theology - faith and belief - are so difficult to grasp and to really hold onto in a tangible, committed way. Of course, we have the theological definition of faith in Hebrews 11:1, but it is very difficult to make the leap from the dishonest world we see and experience on a daily basis into this hoped for and unevidentiary belief in a fair, just, honest, trustworthy God who says He keeps His promises and He is the same yesterday, today, and tomorrow.

And that difficulty can be traced directly to rampant dishonesty and hypocrisy - which is a facet of dishonesty - among the human leaders who claim to represent God. How many of these leaders have said one thing in their pulpits and done something totally different away from there? A parade of names from distant and recent history comes to mind: Aimee Semple McPherson, Garner Ted Armstrong, Jimmy Swaggart, Jim Bakker, Ted Haggard, Eddie Long, and Crefo Dollar, to name a few of the more notorious examples. But beyond these more visible examples, it is hard to look anywhere in the wide world of "religion" and not see extant examples of dishonesty - whether it is outright lying or the more manipulative spinning and twisting of facts and information - and hypocrisy.

But religious denominations and their leaders, it turns out, tend to reflect the world they exist in, instead of reflecting God and His standard of conduct (the Bible). What does that world look like?
It's dishonest, deceitful, and hypocritical. Take a look at advertising and how little we trust it anymore. I have been going through all four seasons of the AMC original series Mad Men and you cannot help but walk away from that without realizing that advertising - both as a profession and as a tool for selling - is the creme dela creme of dishonesty, hypocrisy, and deceit.

One glaring example of this dishonesty lies within a series of Progressive Insurance commercials that is popular right now in the United States. In several of this insurance company's commercials, two insurance agents from "another" insurance company both lie about the products their company offers and endorse the products of Progressive. One action is fraudulent; the other breaks the non-compete clause that most of us sign when we go to work for a company now. Both are dishonest. And yet this dishonesty is not called what it is, but instead is recast as benign bumbling that is humorous.

Here's the irony. We want people to be honest and yet we treat dishonesty as normal and harmless, whether it's our own or others.

In our society, to be a politician - a political leader - being dishonest is a key to success. When a human being promises other human beings to meet each and every of all their needs and wants, that person is being dishonest, because that is impossible to do. The term "flip-flopping," which has become of mainstay of the 2012 United States presidential race, is a euphemism for dishonesty. Political ads are inherently dishonest, based less on fact, and more on twisting and spinning story lines to promote a position or agenda.

Yet, no matter how much we see this during campaigning, it amazes me how shocked we are to find out that presidents routinely lie, whether we find that out while they are in office or years down the road - such as in the case of President Franklin D. Roosevelt, whose debilitating polio and one or more affairs were hidden from the public, and President John F. Kennedy, who also suffered from a debilitating back injury, was a womanizer, involved with the Mafia, and in general a pretty scummy human being.

And organizational leaders lie routinely too. We need look no further than the economy-crashing banking crisis of 2008, the innumerable Ponzi schemes, of which the most visible was Bernie Madoff's, that came to light, and the continued dishonesty that is overtly prevalent in the financial sector (Jamie Dimon and JPMorgan Chase are a recent example of this continuing status quo of dishonesty), but exists in every other organizational sector in the world.

Our economy and our business environment is built on, depends on, and is routinely led by dishonesty and deception.

I know those are strong words, but one of the tenants of being honest is to be honest consistently and continually and that means being unequivocal all the time. It's a tall order, but without it, we will never develop - and this takes conscious effort, because a lot of the time being dishonest and/or deceitful seems like it is a lot easier - the quintessential leader trait of honesty and in turn becoming trustworthy to the teams we lead.

Let's look at some specific examples of what the quintessential leader trait of honesty looks - and doesn't look - like. Maybe a leader is honest with his team not hiding any truth from them. But what if his or her team routinely sees the leader exhibit dishonest behavior outside the confines of the team?
Is the leader honest with his or her superiors, or does the leader routinely fudge, obfuscate, tell "little white lies" (there is no such thing: a lie is a lie is a lie) to them about things? This routinely occurs in most organizations. Sometimes it done under the guise of protecting the team and sometimes it's done out of habit. Either way, it's dishonest.

Is the leader honest with his or her peers or is he or she known to exaggerate or embellish on a regular basis? This is ego-driven dishonesty and comes from a spirit of competition and one-upmanship. This is definitely not a quintessential leader we're talking about, but it reflects a lot of the people we see in leadership positions in organizations.

Does the leader respect company property and use it honestly? For example, if the leader has a company credit card does he or she use it strictly for company/business-related expenses or does the leader do things like put personal expenditures on it from time to time or use it to take everyone out for a night on the town during a business trip? Is their computer, phone, car - and anything else the company might provide - used solely for business or are they routinely employed for the leader's personal use? If company property is used for anything other than directly-related-to-business purposes and things, then those uses are an example of dishonesty.

And here's the net effect of these areas of dishonesty. Even if a leader is honest with his or her team, because he or she is dishonest in every other part of his or her life, the team can't trust him or her. The team will question even the things that are true and will never trust the leader. The evidence is too compelling that, in the balance of things, he or she is untrustworthy.

And without trust, they, you, and I have nothing.

Chapter 3: The Integrity Component of Trust and Trustworthiness

We have already looked in-depth at the honesty component of trust and trustworthiness, and now we will look a corresponding and complementary component: integrity. They are not the same, although both must be present in quintessential leaders. To separate them more logically in thinking, honesty is *how* a person is (conduct), while integrity is *who* and *what* a person is (values and standards).

Generally, one doesn't exist without the other because they depend on each other. If you observe someone who's habitually dishonest with him or herself and others in any and/or every part of his or her life, you will find upon further observation, that person also lacks integrity. On the other hand, if you see someone who's habitually honest with him or herself in any and/or every part of his or her life, upon further observation of that person, you will learn that he or she possesses integrity.

The word *integrity* comes from the root word *integral*, which means, among other things, *entire*, *complete*, or *whole*. And that is a strong part of what integrity actually is. It is undivided and unwavering with regard to moral principles, to right and wrong, to right values and standards.

There is no deviation, regardless of circumstances or costs. It is a systemic quality that affects everything in life. If it's not a part of a person, life is perpetually chaotic, a free-for-all, and completely unpredictable in terms of directions and outcomes. If it is part of a person, there's an unchangeable and dependable framework that can be trusted and counted on no matter what's going on inside the frame.

So, what does integrity look like in action? It first has an intrinsic set of immutable values and standards and adheres to those values and standards, no matter what. Second, it is a conscious and deliberate choice of service - selflessness - over self-interest.

Integrity, by default, is encapsulated by Spock's famous statement before sacrificing his life to save the rest of the Enterprise crew in *The Wrath of Khan*: "The needs of the many outweigh the needs of the one." A quintessential leader will have the integrity to do what's best for everyone, not just what's best for him or herself. There is never a component of self-interest as a guiding principle in decision-making.

Integrity is also demonstrated by good stewardship. A quintessential leader will use resources correctly and judiciously and will acquire and allocate them fairly and skillfully, maximizing the benefit to all, based on needs, not wants.

Additionally, a quintessential leader will guard and protect those resources, ensuring that they are not diluted or wasted (this includes people – a good team can be undone by just one person that is not contributing or is actively creating divisions and disruptions).

Integrity means honoring commitments and keeping promises. In short, it means following through on what you say. A quintessential leader, therefore – and this is another aspect of integrity, must know his or her limitations and abilities to follow through before committing to and promising things. Two of the most frustrating and unquintessential leadership qualities are overcommitting and overpromising and then never fulfilling either. It destroys morale and it destroys trust.

Integrity means aligning actions with beliefs – authenticity. A quintessential leader's actions are always in sync with his or her values, standards and beliefs. There is never any deviation from those in anything he or she does and the repeated demonstration of that syncing builds trust and makes him or her trustworthy.

A quintessential leader demonstrates integrity by consistently communicating his or her values and standards and adhering to those with every person and in every circumstance without exception. Granted, a quintessential leader may have team members who don't share or don't like his or her values and standards, but there will never be any doubt about what they are and that the quintessential leader will always adhere to them and expects his or her teams to adhere to them within the leader/team relationship.

As discussed in my post on Joe Paterno and Penn State, "Absolute Power Corrupts Absolutely," what Joe Paterno and Penn State demonstrated is that he and they lacked integrity. Penn State could have done a lot to repair the reputation of the school if they had, even though this would have still been late in the process, come clean as soon as this whole sordid and shameful mess came to light, admitted their own wrong-doing and complicity, fired Joe Paterno right away, taken down any references and monuments to him, put their entire athletic program on a self-imposed and indefinite moratorium and firing the entire staff of the athletic department, and set up a generous fund for the victims of these crimes as well as commit financially to donate from that point forward to organizations that helped abuse victims.

Instead, the complete lack of integrity is glaringly evident. Denials and accusations toward the victims and supposed-enemies of Paterno and Penn State abounded. The statue of Joe Paterno stood standing until this past Sunday (July 22, 2012) when, just ahead of the Monday (July 23, 2012) announcement by the NCAA of their sanctions against the school, it was removed. The very fact that an outside body – the NCAA – had to decide Penn State's fate from 1998 until now, vacating all of Paterno's wins during those years, and moving forward is a testament to the lack of integrity that permeates Penn State even in the absence of Paterno. It's a sad testimony.

Quite frankly, I think the NCAA let Penn State off too easily. They should have shuttered the whole school for good (I realize they could not have done that all by themselves, but it could have been done with the cooperation of the Pennsylvania and US government by cutting off all state and federal financial, legal, and other support).

Why? Because the school still lacks integrity. Why would parents want their children graduating from a university where a lack of integrity is an intrinsic part of its culture? It isn't a huge leap to assume that Penn State's athletic department and executive staff are the only entities lacking integrity. Anyone in any position with Penn State should be considered suspect in having integrity. Is that what parents want their kids to graduate from college possessing, having been immersed in a culture of it for four or more years?
I would certainly hope not.

Chapter 4: The Fairness Component of Trust and Trustworthiness

In this chapter, we will talk about another component of trust and trustworthiness: fairness.

In this chapter, we'll examine what fairness is and what it isn't, and we'll also see what it looks like - and doesn't look like - in practice. No one reading this post will not have, at some point or another, not experienced unfairness - a lot of unfairness, I suspect, based on my experience - in the workplace from people in leadership positions. I personally believe that being fair across the board consistently is a hard thing for all of us to do. Because this trait means setting aside our likes and dislikes, personal preferences, and personal feelings about other people, and that strikes at the core of what makes us tick as people and how we bond or don't bond with each other.

There is no simple definition of fairness, but it can best be described as having objective standards and rules that apply - and are applied - to everyone across the board without exception and being unbiased and unprejudiced in dealing with all people. Quintessential leaders must have this trait in order to earn trust and to become trustworthy, because people will always respond favorably - even when there is a negative consequence for non-adherence - to someone who doesn't bend the rules, play favorites, or have different sets of standards and rules for different people or groups of people.

The reality is we all encounter issues with fairness very early in life. Often we first experience it within our families, where consciously or unconsciously, parents may have a "favorite" child and that child seemingly can do no wrong and gets away with murder, so to speak, while the other children are routinely held accountable for adhering to the family rules. This sets up sibling rivalry, which can have devastatingly divisive consequences for the family far into the future.

We next experience it our extra-familial settings: school, sports, church, clubs, etc. We've all seen this first-hand in the form of teachers' pets, the star athletes, pastors' kids (PK's), and within social and civic clubs like Boy Scouts, Girl Scouts, etc. If we weren't among any of these groups of people, then we often saw and experienced first-hand the unfairness of treatment. Teachers' pets, for example, never had to write "I will not talk in class." 500 times, while we, even if we weren't talking, had to write the hand-numbing sentences along with the people who were actually talking.

Star athletes could flagrantly break all the team rules and still be on the team and playing, while we, if we broke just one and were caught, were either suspended for several games or kicked off the team altogether. Pastors' kids - and I have a lot of good friends who grew up PK's, so I'm not picking on them because they're pretty acutely aware of both the preferential treatment they received as well as the fishbowl scrutiny they lived under - were often the wildest kids in church, yet they were not punished, while most of us, if we broke the rules and got caught, had the heavy hand of punishment dropped on us like a ton of bricks.

And in our adult lives, we experience the same kind of unfairness in the workplace. We watch colleagues, who are friends with or liked by their superiors, get special advantages, promotions that are not related to ability and suitability, and no consequences for circumventing or breaking organizational rules and policies or for doing illegal and immoral things. We have worked among brown-nosers and suck-ups who take advantage of the lack of fairness that is prevalent  among many people who are in leadership positions and we watch them rise through the ranks, not on merit or hard work, but because of their attachment or affiliation with upper management. In the South, for example, there seems to be an unwritten law that, regardless of experience and qualifications, a person will not gain employment with an organization unless he or she is "from around here," is related to someone in the organization, knows someone well-placed in the organization, or is friends with someone well-placed in the organization.

In my personal experience, I worked for one organization where unfairness was so in-your-face that the only people who got called on the carpet regularly and when they left the organization had the door slammed on any future employment were the people who were honest, worked hard, and met all the organizational policies, standards and rules, while the people who were dishonest, slackers, and met none of the organizational policies, standards and rules were never called on any of it and were assured of future employment - many times over - no matter under what circumstances - theft, drug use, etc. - they left the organization previously.

So we see that there are a lot of parents, coaches, preachers, teachers, and employers who are not quintessential leaders because they lack this essential component of fairness. They all have one thing in common: they have double-standards based on their subjective and personal relationships with those entrusted to their care.

Quintessential leaders distinguish themselves, then, by objectively applying a single standard to everyone and by making decisions based on objective factors - merit, ability, strengths, weaknesses, performance and suitability - rather than whether they like or don't like, know or don't know, are friends with or not friends with everyone whose paths intersect with theirs.

They treat everyone the same and they give everyone who meets basic qualifications the same opportunities and chances to succeed and move forward. They don't do anything based on personality or likability, but instead use the same criteria for everything and everyone all the time.

It may mean promoting someone the leader doesn't particularly care for on a personal level, but sees how that person can move the team forward to greater success. It may mean more interaction and coaching with an under-performer, who wants to perform better but just doesn't have the skills and tools to do it (it is much easier to spend time with great performers who get great results and grow by leaps and bounds).

It may mean enforcing negative consequences on a well-liked and valued team member or friend when he or she steps outside the boundaries of organizational policies, rules, and standards. It may even mean terminating a well-liked and valued team member or friend when the infractions are repeated or even escalate to a criminal level.

That's the tough part of fairness, and yet without this component, a person will never be a quintessential leader and will never be trusted and considered trustworthy.

Chapter 5: The Righting Wrongs Component of Trust and Trustworthiness

This chapter is one in which we'll tackle a subject that addresses the heart of a quintessential leader. It is true that no one really knows our hearts completely except for God. However, behavior (actions and words) indicates the state of our character (good or bad) and character indicates the state of our inner selves - the heart.

I believe one of the most difficult things for all of us to do is to admit we made a mistake, we were wrong, or we screwed up. There is something intrinsic in us that wants to avoid that, deny that, excuse that, justify that, or even blame it on someone else. This reticence to own up, to take responsibility for all of our words and actions will be addressed fully in an upcoming chapter on another of the components of trust and trustworthiness, which is accountability.

But the fact that we all wrestle with the admission of wrong-doing, in whatever form those words and/or actions took - and until we admit wrong-doing, we cannot right wrong-doing - shows that this is a quintessential leader trait we must be consciously working to both acquire and practice consistently. Without it, we will not be quintessential leaders.

There are many examples of the fallout from being unwilling to admit and then to right wrongs that we can look at to see, as quintessential leaders, what not to do. I will briefly summarize a few here, but I strongly encourage you to research on your own the many more examples from history, religion, society, and public life where wrongs were not admitted to and corrected to see how devastating the results were and to understand the things that each of us must be on guard to not repeat in our own lives and leadership of others. I also strongly encourage each of us to look at our own lives for examples where we have not exhibited this quintessential leader trait.

Unfortunately, we all have them. We may not be in a position to go back and fix them all - if we are, we should - but we have the opportunity to learn the lessons and change so that we are consistently admitting, without excuses and blame, and righting our wrongs immediately.

There are two examples of people in leadership positions who lacked this quintessential leader trait in the Bible that stand out in my mind every time I read about them and I literally shake my head that they were unwilling to do anything about it, even though the consequences were dire and long-term.

One is the high priest Eli (I Samuel 2:12-36 through I Samuel 3:1-18). Despite being told twice about the sins of his sons and the wrongs he needed to right, he made little effort to actually correct them and actually dismissed them in the end with an indifferent statement to the effect of "what will be, will be." From that point on, all his male descendants died in their prime and none lived to see old age. They were also cut off from automatic ascension to the priesthood.

The second example from the Bible is that of King Hezekiah after his life is extended 15 years (II Kings 20:12-24). Instead of admitting his mistake and correcting it, like Eli, his attitude is "what will be will be," but he goes a step further to reveal the fact that he was not in any shape or form a quintessential leader by saying out loud, even though his unwillingness to right the wrong would lead to destruction of his kingdom and would affect his children horribly and personally, "well, it won't happen in my lifetime, so who cares?"

There are also many public figures in positions of leadership, past and present, who lacked this quintessential leader trait and the results were devastating to a lot of people.

One en masse example of this is the persistent "we weren't responsible" mantra of banking executives regarding their culpability in the Great Recession that began in 2008. There is a continual denial that they personally dropped the ball of oversight over the financial institutions they were responsible for leading and an equally continual finger-pointing at politicians and consumers as the perpetrators of the financial collapse. The reality is much different than the picture they portray in which they cast themselves as victims, since the blame lies with all the parties involved and greed was the underlying motivation.

Another recent example of failing to admit wrongs and correcting them was BP's chief executive Tony Hayward after the 2010 Gulf of Mexico oil spill. Hayward spent almost five months denying any responsibility by BP for the spill, instead casting the blame far and wide to subcontractors and circumstances outside BP's control, and refusing to accept any liability for cleanup and compensation for the spill.

The denials and blame-game became a public relations nightmare for BP, who finally replaced Hayward in October 2010 with another chief executive. These are just a few public examples of the lack of the quintessential leader trait of righting wrongs.

The lack of this character-defining component of quintessential leadership, though, exists in every part of the human experience where leadership should exist: families, where spouses and parents don't own up to and correct wrongs in their own lives and with each other and their children; schools, where principals and teachers don't admit and fix mistakes and errors; religious organizations, where clergy and people in administrative leadership positions refuse to acknowledge wrongs and take action to right those wrongs; secular organizations, where people in leadership positions ignore or deny mistakes and issues and nothing is done to correct them.

None of us who is in a leadership position is immune to the tendency to refuse to admit and right wrongs. It seems to me to be one of those battleground areas of our character and of being a quintessential leader where we have to stay vigilantly aware, humbly conscious, and continuously fighting to not fail.

<u>Why is it so important to admit wrongs and mistakes quickly and fix and right them just as quickly</u>? Because not doing so creates relationship problems that are not easily - and, in some cases, can never be completely - remedied and overcome. What do the results of this look like?

- Creates a breach in the relationship(s)
- Creates a total lack of trust
- Engenders a lack of respect
- Destroys closeness of relationship(s)
- Destroys cohesiveness of relationship(s)
- Destroys connectivity of relationship(s)
- Sets a negative example for those we lead

If we are not actively acquiring and doing this component of trust and trustworthiness, then we are not quintessential leaders. In fact, we're not leaders at all. Instead, we are failures in every part of our lives. That's how important this is. And that is why it must be uppermost in our character and consciousness always.

Chapter 6: The Accountability Component of Trust and Trustworthiness

This chapter will talk about another component of trust and trustworthiness: accountability.

In this chapter we'll show the aspects that encompass accountability and I believe it will become apparent when we review those that there is a serious lack of quintessential leadership in all walks of life today. But as we strive to be quintessential leaders, we will see that the component of accountability is one that must be part of who and what we are in order to build trust and be trustworthy.

What does accountability entail and how does accountability get measured in terms of quintessential leadership? Merriam-Webster defines accountability as "an obligation or willingness to accept responsibility" or "to account for one's actions." Being obligated and being willing are both attributes of character and mindset, which are crucial areas of distinction that make quintessential leaders stand out from everyone else.

Obligation is rarely found in organizational thinking today and in many ways it reflects the larger lack of a sense of obligation reflected in society. Instead of recognition and actions that reflect that recognition of what we owe others, society, in general, has adopted an entitlement mindset that says "I owe nothing, but everyone else owes me." This is reflected in the "I deserve" and "my rights" attitudes that are prevalent in every part of life - home, family, school, extracurricular activities, religion, and work - today.

Obligation, by definition, is not negotiable. It is an integral and driving force in who we are, what we do, what we say, and how we think. Quintessential leaders know and understand their obligations and strive to fulfill them in every part of their lives and that includes the area of accountability.
Willingness is another character and mindset attribute of a quintessential leader.

Even if people know they should (obligation) do something, but they don't do it, then they lack the quality of willingness. There is a proverb that says the road to hell is paved with good intentions. This speaks directly to knowing we should do something, but being unwilling, whether by procrastination, slothfulness, or lack of desire, to do what we know we should do.

So, as quintessential leaders, we know we should and are willing to be accountable for everything within our control. What does that exactly mean? What does it look like in practice?

Mike Myatt, in his article, "Leadership is Not Dodgeball," gives a big-picture summary in his title. We all remember playing dodge ball in elementary school. The object of the game was to avoid being hit by the ball if you were in the middle of the circle and it required running, jumping out of the way, ducking, and occasionally pushing other people in the path of the ball. And for the most part, we see people in leadership positions doing these same maneuvers in terms of accountability in negative situations (these are also the first people to take full credit and accountability in positive situations).

One of the most common responses of most people in leadership positions today, across the human spectrum of organizational units and constructs when problems, issues, and mistakes happen is to simply run away - to distance themselves personally as far from the negative events as possible. This is out and out cowardice and not a quintessential leader trait.

If running away doesn't get the heat off them, then comes the ducking and dodging, which manifests itself as spin, twisting facts, diverting attention (straw men arguments), outright lies, and vociferous denials (as soon as I personally see this stage emerge, Shakespeare's famous line from *Hamlet* - "The lady doth protest too much, methinks." - comes to mind).

And if all of those fail, then comes the blame game, where everyone and everything possibly imaginable - and this can get so fanciful and unbelievable that people would literally have to suspend all reason, logic, and common sense to believe, but incredibly, there are always some who can do that - is at fault except for those in leadership positions.

So now that we've seen what no accountability looks like, let's see what the quintessential leader trait of being accountable looks like in practice. Quintessential leaders take full responsibility and ownership for everything within their care and control.

When problems, issues, and mistakes happen, as was discussed earlier in this book when we discussed the component of righting wrongs, quintessential leaders first admit that something that was entrusted to them failed to meet expectations or simply failed and they take full responsibility for that failure. In both the ownership and the fix - which is righting the wrong - a quintessential leader will exclusively use the pronoun "I" instead of "we" and/or "they."

Taking ownership requires courage, and being accountable means accepting both responsibility and the consequences for mistakes, bad decisions - as long as we all breathe for a living, we will have bad decisions as part of our experience, because none of us is perfect - problems and issues.

The other side of the coin of ownership and accountability beyond owning our mistakes, issues, problems, and bad decisions is to understand and explain why we made them, what we learned (and this is key - one of the things I tell the people I lead is "every mistake is a learning opportunity to know what not to do again"), and what changes we will make to address and correct them.

Even if other people don't practice accountability, they will respect someone who does. Our teams will respect and value our leadership if we consistently demonstrate our personal accountability in everything we are and do.

For most of us as quintessential leaders, we do not have a safe environment in which to fail (this is often a factor in the overwhelming lack of accountability we see at all levels in every walk of life), but our character and mindset does not let this deter us from always striving to do the right thing.

It is important, though, that we offer that safe environment for the people we lead to fail and coach them through the failures to see and understand why and to come up with workable strategies to fix what is broken and then to change and grow so that the failures aren't repeated. The reality is we have a window of opportunity to teach those we lead to become accountable and we should not forget to take those opportunities to coach and grow future quintessential leaders.

Chapter 7: The Consistency Component of Trust and Trustworthiness

This chapter will talk about the trust and trustworthiness component of consistency. In this post we'll discuss why consistency is an integral part of building trust and being trustworthy. We will also discuss key areas that reveal either consistency or a lack of consistency.

Merriam-Webster defines consistency in part as "harmony of conduct or practice with profession." What this means in practical terms is that a quintessential leader is who he or she says he or she is and that he or she is what he or she says they believe - all the time, without exception. When we as quintessential leaders practice consistency, our teams always know what to expect and that helps to create an organized, sensible and predictable environment in which team members can operate, grow, and thrive.

When those who claim to be leaders don't practice consistency, they become very much like Robert Louis Stevenson's Dr. Jekyll and Mr. Hyde. The environment for their teams is chaotic, confusing and unpredictable and is characterized by constant fear and failure to thrive.

Consistency, like all the other components of trust and trustworthiness, is a rare commodity in any part of life today. It goes hand-in-hand with fairness and character. In society, in parenting, in politics, in religion, and in business, consistency has been replaced by expediency. The lack of consistency that overshadows humanity now is also a reflection of the "it's all about me" mindset that seems to be the driving force in most people today.

Convictions, commitments, principles are built on foundations of sand that shift continuously (and are, therefore, broken almost as soon as they are made) depending on the situation at the moment. Most people and most people in leadership positions are more concerned about how things will effect them personally and how things look than they are about consistency, fairness, and character.

That is a sad commentary on what we as a society have become. However, quintessential leaders don't follow the crowd and allow society to mold and shape them ("everybody else is doing it, so it must be okay"), but instead stay on the path of building trust and being trustworthy and they exhibit consistency no matter what the situation both as leaders and examples to others.

I was recently at a conference where I saw a lot of glaring examples of inconsistency among people in leadership positions. But one stood out more than most of the others. A presenter had three presentations during the conference. In his first presentation, he made some erroneous and unsupported statements that left many of us scratching our heads. In his second presentation, he was on target with everything and was able to fully provide support for the whole presentation. In his third presentation, he went back to the erroneous and unsupported statements of the first presentation and actually expanded on them.

The problem? The speaker's second presentation completely contradicted what he said in his first and third presentations.

The lack of consistency was apparent immediately. But even more apparent was his lack of trustworthiness. I found myself asking "what does this person really believe?" Because his middle presentation completely disagreed with his first and third presentations, I came away with a Dr. Jekyll/Mr. Hyde impression of him.

Clearly, a sane, sensible, logical person could not hold both of the viewpoints he presented at the same time. So who was he? The person in the first and third presentations? Or the person in the second presentation? Or none of the above? And even though the statements in this speaker's first and third presentations were erroneous and unsupported, if he had maintained them in his second presentation, he would have been consistent and everyone would have known exactly where he stood.

Instead, nobody knows where this speaker stands really and he lost all credibility with me because of his inconsistency. I don't trust him become he was inconsistent.

What key areas, then, are crucial to the quintessential leader trait of consistency?

Actions, attitudes, and motivations must match words. In other words, quintessential leaders don't just talk the talk, but they walk the walk. The real measure of who anyone is at his or her very core is what he or she does. A quintessential leader doesn't give lip service to values, principles, commitments and convictions, but instead lives them, all the time, no matter what.

Another area of consistency in a quintessential leader is vision, priorities, and decisions. In other words, a quintessential leader never takes his or her eye off the big-picture and always aligns personal and team priorities and decisions with that goal. There is no flip-flopping, no wishy-washiness, no spur-of-the-moment "better offer" that gets in the way of that or sidetracks and derails him or her from it.

Consistency in a quintessential leader means keeping commitments and promises, no matter how difficult or inconvenient at times that may be. In the chapter that covered the integrity component, we discussed how critical knowing our limitations and ability to fulfill commitments and promises is to our actually making them. The disappointment and damage from an unfulfilled commitment or promise is devastatingly permanent, while the letdown of having to say "no" to these kinds of requests up front is temporary and, in time, appreciated.

Consistency also encompasses how a quintessential leader treats people. Not all quintessential leaders have job titles that designate them publicly as a leader. But people naturally gravitate toward those around them who treat everyone with respect, kindness, and who have that uncanny ability to encourage and constructively advise to correction - without it seeming like correction - everyone with whom they come in contact with. There is no partiality, no favoritism, no injustice, no variability.

Consistency is hard for us all to maintain. We all have "good" and "bad" days and "right" and "wrong" thinking and attitudes at times. As quintessential leaders, we must be in a continual mode of objective and in-depth self-examination of our words, our actions, our thoughts, our motivations, who and what we are at our cores, to first ensure that we are on the path of building trust and being trustworthy and then ensuring that we are being consistent everywhere along that path.

Chapter 8: The Sincerity Component of Trust and Trustworthiness

This chapter discusses another component of trust and trustworthiness: sincerity.

A lack of sincerity has been painfully and increasingly evident in business, political, educational, civil, and religious leadership for quite some time, and it's becoming the norm instead of the exception. While sincerity is very closely aligned with honesty, integrity, and authenticity, it is still a distinct component from these other quintessential leadership traits.

Sincerity, put simply, is the opposite of hypocrisy. But we need to define both of those words to see why.

Hypocrisy, in its simplest definition, is a person pretending to be, do, or believe something he or she isn't, doesn't do, or doesn't believe. The Greek root of this word means "play-acting." In other words, a hypocrite is faking it or perpetuating fraud.

Sincerity, on the other hand, defines a person who actually is, does, and believes everything he or she appears to be, does, and says he or she believes. In other words, a sincere person is "for real," genuine, and free of pretense and deceit. Sincerity, then, is a quintessential leader trait and another key component of building trust and being trustworthy.

What sets the component of sincerity apart from honesty, integrity, and authenticity, although, again it is closely related to all of these, is that it indicates a person's motives or motivations. This is another aspect of character - a heart issue. The other side of the coin, hypocrisy, also speaks to motives, motivations, and character.

No where recently have we seen hypocrisy abound and sincerity questioned than in the aftermath of Hurricane Sandy, which left a wide and extensive swath of devastation when it merged with two other storms to form a super-storm over the northeast United States on October 29-30, 2012.

The first news of a hypocritical posture was the juxtaposition of then-presidential-candidate Mitt Romney's previous statements about the Federal Emergency Management Agency (FEMA), when he said it wasn't needed, and his statements this week saying FEMA was needed.

It's impossible, because of this potential leader's lack of sincerity - he said, when it looked politically expedient (motive) for him to do so and has done this same sort of thing repeatedly as a matter of course during his 2012 presidential campaign, something this week that completely disagreed with what he has said before – to know where he really stands on this and many of the other issues and positions he has flip-flopped on throughout his years as a politician.

If he really doesn't know what he believes and just goes whichever way the wind blows, then he is not a quintessential leader, and if he does know what he believes but is willing to pretend he believes something else to gain votes, then he's a hypocrite.

The next person's whose sincerity – and character – came under scrutiny was Chris Christie's, the Republican governor of New Jersey, when he worked closely with and had high praise for President Obama's and FEMA's response and help immediately after the storm. (President Obama's sincerity was also brought into question, ridiculously and illogically, as I read editorials that somehow suggested he had masterminded the storm so he could have a crisis to look like a quintessential leader in order to try to win re-election next week.)

Although I take exception to Chris Christie's unquintessential leader trait of bullying at times, in the big scheme of things he displays a lot of quintessential leader traits, and it was clear during the aftermath of Hurricane Sandy that he was taking his role as governor of New Jersey seriously and wanted to help his state and its citizens. The media questioned the sincerity of that goal almost immediately as they looked for hidden motives about Governor Christie positioning himself for the 2016 presidential election by his words and actions.

The reality is that Governor Christie was doing the job he was entrusted with and that was taking care of New Jersey and its residents. He didn't and is not wavering from that. Period. Whether the man inspires or offends you, he is being sincere and this is consistent with what I've read, seen, and know of him as a quintessential leader and as a person.

Sincerity, then, it appears makes people, at times uncomfortable, and because there is so little of it evident in any sector of leaders, it has become an alien concept to the very people - and everyone else, for that matter - that it should be familiar to and part of their character.

Michael Bloomberg, mayor of New York City, is much harder to read and his sincerity - or the lack of it - are more questionable. An Independent (he is neither a Republican nor a Democrat), Mayor Bloomberg endorsed President Obama for re-election in 2012.

Well, sort of. Kind of.

In his statement, in which he stated climate change legislation as the reason for his endorsement, Mayor Bloomberg also said "If the 1994 or 2003 version of Mitt Romney were running for president, I may well have voted for him because, like so many other independents, I have found the past four years to be, in a word, disappointing."

This statement shows a lack of sincerity on Mayor Bloomberg's part. Additionally, he is endorsing President Obama for re-election based on a single, hotly-debated issue that even scientists and geologists can't agree on.

In the big picture of time, Hurricane Sandy is not the strongest hurricane (and Bloomberg fails to recognized that it merged with two other storms coming from the west, which gave it its punch) to ever hit the northeast, nor does the NOAA hurricane data indicate that the relative warmth of 2012 made this an unusual year for hurricanes in general, since much stronger and more frequent storms (the 1950's were particularly severe for the Atlantic coast) have been recorded.

Why would you endorse a presidential candidate for his position on a side-bar (in the larger context) issue when you think the rest of his term is "disappointing?" Like Mitt Romney, it's impossible to tell exactly where Mayor Bloomberg stands because he lacks sincerity in conviction, in substance, and in belief.

We, as quintessential leaders, need to be constantly examining our motives and motivations and ensure that we are being sincere in every aspect of our lives. Without sincerity, we will build no trust and we will not be trustworthy.

Chapter 9: The Setting Boundaries Component of Trust and Trustworthiness

This chapter discusses another component of building trust and being trustworthiness. That component is setting boundaries.

In this chapter, we'll look at what setting boundaries encompasses and what it means in practical terms and why it is so important for quintessential leaders to do. We will also examine how this component affects, negatively or positively, depending on whether it's both done and adhered to, not only organizations and teams, but individuals in leadership positions themselves.

Setting boundaries is often misunderstood as a set of hard and fast do's and don'ts or rigid rules that are put in place, and tyrannical and <u>bullying</u> people in leadership positions using these as hammers over the heads of the people who report to them. Think <u>J. Edgar Hoover</u> and <u>the FBI</u>. Think <u>Richard Nixon</u> and <u>Watergate</u>. Think <u>George Steinbrenner</u>, <u>Billy Martin</u>, and the <u>New York Yankees</u>. Think <u>Jerry Jones</u> and the <u>Dallas Cowboys</u>.

Setting boundaries involves parameters, expectations, principles, ethics, right and wrong. The ability to set boundaries and to uphold and maintain, without exception, those boundaries is a mark of true leadership and a mark of quintessential leadership. It is the opposite of compromise in any of these areas. It is another aspect of character and integrity.

None of us need to look very far around us to see that there are very few people in the world who are able to or will set, uphold, and maintain boundaries as described above. Almost everything and everyone in society, in parenting, in politics, in religion, and in business has become situational instead of absolute in terms of parameters, expectations, ethics, principles, and right and wrong. Let's look first at the area of parameters and expectations and see why setting boundaries here is so important and what the impact is when boundaries are not set.

Parameters are guiding lines for a course of action. For example, when we drive on a road, there are white solid lines that reflect light at night on each side of the road. If the road is an interstate, drivers' lanes are delineated by dashed white lines on the road. If it is a two-lane road, the middle double yellow lines, which also reflect light at night, are either solid or solid and dashed.

These are parameters for us when we are driving. We know where the edges of the road are by the white solid lines on either side. If we're driving on the interstate, we know where our lanes are by the white dashed lines. If we're driving on a two-lane road, we know which side of the road we're supposed to stay on and whether it's safe to pass another car or not by the yellow lines down the middle of the road. These lines guide our driving behavior. We all are well aware of the sad and tragic results when a driver, for whatever reason, does not stay within these parameters.

Parameters within the rest of life serve the same purpose as the guiding lines on the road. They tell us where we're supposed to be and what we can do within that space. When quintessential leaders set the boundary of parameters, they free up their team members to grow and be creative within a well-defined framework.

Like the lanes on a road, it is not a tight fit, but instead an area designed to handle a lot of different possibilities, skills, ideas, temperaments, and personalities. But each of those must stay within the definition of the lane.

Setting boundaries in terms of expectations is critical to success within any structural setting. How many of us have been involved in something - family, school, athletics, religious organization, or work - where there were no expectations set or the expectations were unclear or fluid?

As an example of what this looks and sounds like, I had someone who was once in a leadership position over me tell me over and over "I don't know what I want, but I'll know it when I see it." I quit that job in my mind that day before I walked out of his office, because I knew working with him would be nothing but beating my head against a brick wall and it would have a very detrimental effect on me.

Setting Boundaries

I suspect we all have experienced this at some point in our lives. It is the most disconcerting place to be, because you end up wandering aimlessly, hoping that you'll hit the target once and a while, but because there isn't one or it keeps changing, all your efforts end up in failure. Without clear and unchanging expectations, high morale and the strong desire to keep trying to do anything ceases to exist. Hopelessness, frustration, fear, and eventually quitting altogether are the inevitable outcomes.

Setting boundaries in the areas of principles, ethics, and right and wrong deals with acceptable behavior and the consequences of unacceptable behavior. Again, all around us we see that there are few quintessential leaders anywhere in our lives. We consistently see most people are willing - in fact, eager - to make exceptions to and compromise with principles, ethics, and right and wrong depending on the situations they find themselves in.
Quintessential leaders set boundaries in principles, ethics, and right and wrong for themselves and for those they lead. There are no exceptions, no times, no

reasons, when it is ever okay to go outside those boundaries. For themselves. For the teams they lead. Everyone is held to the same standards and everyone is accountable for the consequences if he or she does not meet those standards. This also encompasses another component of trust and trustworthiness, which is fairness. There are no double standards.

When a clear boundary of principles, ethics, of right and wrong doesn't exist, then chaos ensues. Everyone decides for themselves what is principled, what is ethical, what is right and wrong, and everyone does what is right in their own eyes. There is no codified standard to which everyone is held and is accountable for maintaining. Nothing is absolute, so everything is open to personal interpretation, again, depending on the situation, as to whether it's principled, ethical, or right or wrong. You probably know this by a more familiar all-inclusive term: "situational ethics."

One of the most puzzling things I see when there are no boundaries with regard to principles, ethics, and right and wrong is how quick the situational ethicists in leadership positions are to get upset and angry when they are the victims of situational ethics. Suddenly, a very clear boundary of principles, ethics, right and wrong applies to everyone _except_ them.

And, yet, they miss the point that they, by their examples, have set the standard of acceptable behavior by their own behavior. They don't expect any negative consequences from their behavior - generally, there's a good bit of vanity about their exploits are outside principles, ethics, and right and wrong and much of that is in how they got away with it - and there are no or inconsistent consequences for the same kind of behavior from the people who report to them.

Setting boundaries is an essential component of trust-building and being trustworthy. Quintessential leaders already have set all these boundaries in their own lives and strive to uphold and maintain them on a consistent basis.

When they set boundaries for their teams, it creates a safety zone, a stable environment, and it creates a level of integrity and character that is unassailable in that organization, that team, and those team members.

This goes a long way to contribute to overall success and survival organizationally because this is so rare that it will easily stand out from the organizational crowd, and the same benefits experienced internally will be experienced externally.

After all, one of the results of quintessential leadership should be a long-term, unwavering, demonstrable record and pattern of success. Having trust and being trustworthy is the foundation on which that success must be laid.

Chapter 10: The Setting A Higher Standard Component of Trust and Trustworthiness

This chapter talks about another component of trust and trustworthiness: setting a higher standard. We will discuss what that means both in terms of performance, but more importantly, in terms of conduct, and why this is a quintessential trait and why this contributes to building trust and being trustworthy.

I've thought deeply about this component for quite some time as I've, over the course of the last few years, observed in almost every area of life - families, politics, education, religion, military, business, society, and in many individual lives, not only the absence of a higher standard of performance and conduct, but increasingly, no-standard of performance and conduct. It seems that the "anything goes" philosophy has become the norm in the world.

It has, with the recent US presidential election, a very thought-provoking article entitled "General Failure," in this month's (November 2012) issue of The Atlantic - which was written well before the revelation of General David Patraeus's adultery with his biographer and the possible adultery of General John R. Allen with Jill Kelly - and now the resignation of General Patraeus from being CIA director, come back full-force into my line of vision.

This kind of behavior (all the parties know each other and are closely linked to each other) among the powerful in Washington, DC, based on what I've read and heard about it, is not only commonplace, but is seen as acceptable.

The initial reactions from people in leadership positions - Senator Dianne Feinstein (D-California), for example, who implied that General Patraeus should not have resigned because he committed adultery - made it evident that not only are people in leadership positions not setting a higher standard for performance and conduct, but there is, in fact, no standard.

It seems to me that before we talk about setting higher standards in terms of performance and conduct, we need to talk about adultery and why it falls into the higher standard category on a personal and leadership level. Marriage vows are taken based on the trust of two people in each other. By their very nature, they create a trust relationship.

By entering a marriage covenant, both parties are setting, demanding, and promising to adhere to a higher standard of conduct. When either party to those vows, which are made traditionally before God and people, breaks them, that person breaks the trust relationship.

Frankly, if a spouse shows untrustworthiness and destroys the trust in his or her closest personal relationship in life, then he or she is untrustworthy and destroys trust in every part of his or her life.

People in leadership positions who do not set, demand, and adhere to a higher set of standards in performance and conduct are not quintessential leaders. In fact, they are not leaders at all. They are just stand-ins, fillers, wanna be's, pretenders that seem to represent how humanity has become willing to accept anything rather than expect the best in those who aspire to lead.

The article in *The Atlantic*, which shows the lack of setting a higher standard - and quintessential leadership - in the military for performance in promoting generals, removing generals from command positions when they fail to meet those standards, and how it's affected the outcomes of the Vietnam War and the wars in Afghanistan and Iraq, points, in a dramatic way, especially in black and white terms of casualties (dead and wounded), to the literal cost of not setting, demanding, and adhering to a higher standard of performance.

The article does a good job of contrasting how the American military has handled its last three out of four wars with how it handled World War II. It shows how the military academies and the military itself has accepted mediocrity as its standard for leadership.

The military, however, is just one reflection of the larger problem of a lack of setting a higher standard of performance within society.

I had an interesting conversation a few months ago with close friends who serve in the ministry of the church - and who are striving to meet a higher standard of performance and conduct and for whom I could easily do a favorable performance review because I see it in action in both of them constantly and consistently - and when I asked whether there was a performance standards, performance objectives, and performance reviews process for the ministry in place, they replied "they're (the administrative team) working on it."

That struck me as odd because those standards are already defined by God - and, yes, they're high - in I Timothy 3. Goals and outcomes are not that complicated: how are you spending your time and at what level are you doing not just your job, but fulfilling your calling from God? That's measurable in terms of time, level of commitment to serving a congregation spiritually (how much time and effort is put into preparing - researching, studying, etc. - and presenting sermons and Bible studies that guide the congregation into a deeper understanding of the practical application of God's word, law, and way of life; provide topics and sermon notes to quantify) and physically (proactively offering and giving comfort, help, and fulfilling needs as they arise; provide examples to quantify).
How else can it be determined whether ministers are meeting the higher standard that God expects of them in performance? And if they're not, what action needs to be taken to get their performance level to that standard?

Quintessential leaders and leadership make setting, demanding, and adhering to a higher standard of performance the first priority in leading their teams, not something they implement years down the road after everyone's grown accustomed to doing things however each individual thinks or believes it should be done. Not having this as the first goal in assuming leadership positions means a lack of quintessential leadership.

Setting a higher standard of conduct is a complementary part of quintessential leadership. It goes hand-in-hand with setting boundaries, but represents evidentiary boundaries of character in speech and action in all areas of life. It means living and being consistently and inclusively above reproach. It requires a careful consciousness of behavior at all times and a continual attention to maintaining the higher standards. When a person gets careless about standards of conduct, they lose trust and they destroy trustworthiness.

Quintessential leaders stand out from the crowd because they set, demand, and strive to adhere to - we all fall short in this area at times - a higher standard of performance and conduct. They set the example of what it looks like and a quintessential leader, when he or she does fall short, will immediately take responsibility (being accountable) and take whatever action is necessary to right his or her wrong(s) so that trust and trustworthiness aren't destroyed.

Take some time today to look in your leadership mirror and ask yourself if you're setting, demanding, and striving to adhere to a higher standard in performance and conduct for yourself and for those you lead. This is a daily must for quintessential leaders, and if the answer at any point is "no," then take the corrective action to get back on the quintessential leadership track.

www.ingramcontent.com/pod-product-compliance
Lightning Source LLC
Chambersburg PA
CBHW081246170526
45165CB00009B/3213